IRISH
AND PROUD OF IT

EILEEN FITZGERALD

summersdale

IRISH AND PROUD OF IT

Summersdale Publishers Ltd
46 West Street
Chichester
West Sussex
PO19 1RP
UK

www.summersdale.com

Printed and bound in the Czech Republic

ISBN: 978-1-84953-522-9

Substantial discounts on bulk quantities of Summersdale books are available to corporations, professional associations and other organisations. For details contact Nicky Douglas by telephone: +44 (0) 1243 756902, fax: +44 (0) 1243 786300 or email: nicky@summersdale.com.

CONTENTS

INTRODUCTION

From the World Heritage Site of the Boyne Valley to the Ring of Kerry, stopping off en route to sink a few cheeky pints of Guinness at the Storehouse, nipping back to County Clare to dangle your feet off the Cliffs of Moher, this little book will take you on a tour of everything that makes this great country beautiful.

There is no finer place to be proud of than Ireland. So, what are you waiting for? Come and join us on a magical journey through the land of Gulliver, Guinness and the Gaelic, and discover what makes people Irish… and proud of it!

MAKING HISTORY

IMPORTANT DATES IN OUR HISTORY

One of the most important dates in Irish history was around **7500 BC**, when people first settled in the region. Up until then the land had been populated by nomadic tribes. Celtic tribes came along around 600–150 BC, bringing with them the Gaelic culture that was to infuse itself within the landscape and the settled peoples.

St Patrick's Day on **17 March** is no longer just a national holiday and feast day in Ireland – the entire western world now celebrates the life of Ireland's most beloved saint, the man who brought Christianity to the island around 430 BC. A popular toast to St Patrick on this special day is: May the roof above you never fall in, and those gathered beneath it never fall out.

The King Henrys of England played a huge part in the history of Ireland. In **October 1171** Henry Plantagenet (Henry II) invaded and established the island as an English colony, known as the 'Lordship of Ireland'. Four hundred years later, Henry VIII 'united' England and Ireland under one crown when Englishmen living in Ireland proclaimed him king of both.

The legendary Battle of the Boyne in **1690** was an important engagement that was to influence the religious beliefs of the nation up to the present day. War had broken out between the two rival claimants to the thrones of England, Ireland and Scotland; Catholic King James and Protestant King William. They clashed at the River Boyne, near Drogheda on the east coast. William won the battle and James returned to exile in France, his hopes of regaining his former powers crushed.

I'm Irish. We
think sideways.
SPIKE MILLIGAN

One of the most tragic events in Irish history was the Great Potato Famine of **1845–1852**. Over a million Irish citizens starved to death due to a potato blight that wiped out ninety per cent of the country's main food staple. Over a third of the population starved and huge numbers of those who tried to emigrate to England, Canada and the USA died in transit due to the appalling conditions on board the vessels.

The rather brief, but very important, Republic of Ireland Act **1948** was signed into law by the Irish parliament on 21 December that year. It was the day that twenty-six counties of Ireland declared themselves the Irish Republic, free of British control. In the Ireland Act of the following year, Britain declared that Ulster (Northern Ireland) would remain a part of the United Kingdom, unless the Parliament of Northern Ireland formally expressed a wish to join a united Ireland.

I was elected by the women
of Ireland, who instead
of rocking the cradle,
rocked the system.

MARY ROBINSON

County Mayo-born Mary Robinson is a modern national icon. In **1990**, she became the seventh president of Ireland and the first female president of the country. She is widely considered to have transformed and revitalised the role of president during her seven-year tenure.

10 April 1998 was the day the Belfast Agreement, or Good Friday Agreement, was signed – an important step in the peace process and the formal cessation of conflict in Northern Ireland. Some of the major figures to have been party to the agreement were British prime minister Tony Blair, Gerry Adams (president of the Sinn Féin political party), David Trimble (soon to be appointed First Minister of Northern Ireland), Martin McGuinness (later appointed the deputy First Minister of Northern Ireland), John Hume (leader of the Social Democratic and Labour Party), Northern Ireland Secretary Mo Mowlam, and Bertie Ahern, the then Taoiseach of Ireland.

Wherever you go and
whatever you do, may
the luck of the Irish
be there with you.

IRISH PROVERB

On **1 January 2007**, the Irish language became one of the twenty-four official working languages of the European Union. The language is spoken by approximately 130,000 native speakers, has no words for 'yes' or 'no', and contains only eleven irregular verbs (English has over eighty). It was first spoken in Ireland around 300 BC, but by 1800 had ceased to be the language spoken by anyone in Ireland with political power. To this day, around 68,000 households are reported to speak the language on a daily basis.

On **21 March 2009**, the Irish rugby union team won the Six Nations Championship, along with a coveted Grand Slam, when they defeated Wales in Cardiff's Millennium Stadium. It was the first time they had won the championship since 1985 and the first time they had won the Grand Slam since 1948. They returned home to a heroes' welcome.

God is good, but
never dance in
a small boat.

IRISH PROVERB

WE CAN BE HEROES

PEOPLE WE CAN BE PROUD TO CALL OUR OWN

Belfast girl and iconic astrophysicist
Jocelyn Bell Burnell was a postgraduate
student when, in July 1967, she discovered
a 'bit of scruff' on the charts she used
to track stars in the skies – she had
discovered the first radio pulsars, one of
the greatest astronomical discoveries
of the twentieth century. In 2008,
Bell Burnell became the first female
president of the Institute of Physics.

The shamrock, these days, is recognised as the iconic symbol that encapsulates the celebrated 'luck of the Irish'. However, there is a more significant backstory to Ireland's lucky charm. **St Patrick** used the shamrock to teach pagans about the Holy Trinity – the three leaves representing the Father, the Son and the Holy Spirit.

This is one race of people
for whom psychoanalysis
is of no use whatsoever.

SIGMUND FREUD ON THE IRISH

Irish architect **James Hoban** designed America's most iconic building – the White House. In July 1792, seven years after immigrating to the States, Hoban won a design competition for the White House (although some elements, such as the West Wing and the Oval Office, were in fact later additions).

County Offaly-born physicist **George Johnstone Stoney** turned the whole world on to *the* most valuable subatomic elementary particle in the whole of science – the electron (the fundamental quantity unit of electricity). He first introduced the concept in 1874, though he did not devise the word until 1891. Next time you turn your TV or your kettle on, Mr Stoney is the man to thank.

Forget David Beckham. Forget Cristiano Ronaldo. It was Belfast lad **George Best** who had it all; truly great skills coupled with the charisma that made him a worldwide celebrity. Considered the greatest player to ever pull on the green shirt of Northern Ireland, Best spent eleven years playing for Manchester United, with whom he scored 179 goals in 470 matches, won two league titles and starred in the famous 1968 European Cup-winning campaign.

There are only two kinds of people in the world; the Irish and those who wish they were.

IRISH SAYING

Born in County Kildare, **Ernest Shackleton** was unarguably one of the world's great explorers and a leading figure in the so-called 'Heroic Age of Antarctic Exploration'. In January 1909, Shackleton and his team travelled as far south as anyone had managed up to that point. The journey was treacherous, as detailed in his book, *South*, and he was knighted by King Edward VII upon his triumphant return.

Louis Walsh – judge on *The X Factor*, Britain's most-watched TV show of the past decade, has become a true national treasure. Born in County Mayo, Walsh's first job in the music industry was artist management and over the course of his career he has managed Ireland's top talent, including Westlife and Boyzone.

Barry McGuigan – an Irish and international boxing icon – was born in Clones, County Monaghan. Known locally as The Clones Cyclone, McGuigan went on to become the World Boxing Association's Featherweight Champion as well as the BBC's celebrated Sports Personality of the Year in 1985.

It's not that the Irish are cynical. It's rather that they have a wonderful lack of respect for everything and everybody.

BRENDAN BEHAN

The *Guinness World Records* book is now an internationally respected reference book for the planet's greatest and strangest achievements. But its beginnings were far more humble. In 1951, **Hugh Beaver**, the then managing director of Guinness Breweries, went out hunting one day in North Slob, County Wexford, and got into an argument about what the fastest game bird in Europe was. Unable to locate the answer, he set about commissioning what would soon become *The Guinness Book of Records*. It took only four years to become a global publishing icon.

Born and raised in Holywood, County Down, golfer **Rory McIlroy** is one of the youngest and most thrilling players to have achieved major success. Winning the US Open in 2011 and the US PGA championship in 2012, McIlroy is also one of the richest men in sport, reputed to be worth more than $100 million through a combination of winnings and mega sponsorship deals. Go Rory!

An Irishman can be worried
by the consciousness
that there is nothing
to worry about.

AUSTIN O'MALLEY

SOMETHING TO REMEMBER US BY

OUR NATION'S CULTURAL HIGHLIGHTS

The heart of
an Irishman is
nothing but his
imagination.

GEORGE BERNARD SHAW

Located in the beautiful Boyne Valley, the ancient temple at **Newgrange** in County Meath is a one-acre mound shaped like a kidney that is believed to have been constructed over 5,000 years ago (around 3200 BC), making it older than Stonehenge and the Great Pyramid. Built as a place of worship, with many tombs and examples of Neolithic art, archaeologists believed that the temple was the work of an ancient organised society.

The **Ring of Kerry**, on the Iveragh
Peninsula, is a beautiful 179 kilometres
(112-mile) circular tourist route around
County Kerry, south-west Ireland. It
encapsulates everything the world
loves about Ireland – mystic castles,
high-top cliffs, ancient monuments,
spectacular landscapes carved out
of ancient glaciers and famous
archaeological treasures. It even has
some of Europe's best unspoilt beaches.

The sound of Irish seems
to be locked in the
subconscious mind
of our people.

KATE FENNELL

At their highest, the craggy **Cliffs of Moher** in County Clare stand at a massive 214 metres (702 feet) and stretch for 8 kilometres (5 miles) along the Atlantic Ocean. On a clear day, you can see the Aran Islands and Galway Bay, as well as the famous Dingle Peninsula. Over a million tourists visit the area every year – just don't get too close to the edge!

Northern Ireland's most famous natural highlight, the **Giant's Causeway,** is a coastal area of around 40,000 basalt columns near Bushmills, County Antrim – near where the famous Bushmills Irish Whiskey is distilled. Legend tells of a giant called Finn McCool who created the causeway of stones to scare off a rival Scottish giant. In truth, they were created by a super-volcanic eruption 60 million years ago.

Visiting the enthralling **Aran Islands** is like stepping back in time. Situated on the west coast, in Galway Bay, the three remote islands of Inishmore, Inishmaan and Inisheer are famed for their geological formation as well as their preservation of a rural human existence that has remained unchanged for centuries. If you go, be prepared to speak Irish.

We have always
found the Irish
a bit odd.
They refuse to
be English.

WINSTON CHURCHILL

Without a doubt Dublin's most compulsory cultural highlight, the legendary **Guinness Storehouse**, tells the story of how Ireland's proud national drink came to be the country's largest export. Designed around an atrium shaped like a massive pint glass, the building has seven floors dedicated to Guinness history. The Gravity Bar on the top floor has cracking views of Dublin, too. Over a million visitors now stop by each year, many of them having a cheeky one for the road.

The mighty **Burren**, around 250 square
kilometres (97 square miles) in size,
is a giant rocky surface made up of
limestone karst plates. In the summer
it is populated by around 700 different
plant species, including twenty-two of
Ireland's twenty-seven native orchids.
A sight to behold from the air, the word
'Burren' comes from the Irish *Boíreann*,
a rocky place. An astonishing seventy-
five per cent of all of Ireland's native
species grow in the Burren, so tread
carefully if you decide to take a wander.

Every year, over three million people visit Ireland's national (and largest) church, **St Patrick's Cathedral** in Dublin. The current building was largely erected in the thirteenth century, but St Patrick himself baptised people into Christianity on this very site 800 years before that! The cathedral is also revered as the place Handel's *Messiah* was first performed, in 1742.

Ireland's two national sports, hurling and Gaelic football, are played at **Croke Park** stadium, a sacred spiritual home for both sports. With capacity for over 80,000 spectators, it is the fourth-largest stadium in Europe – a massive achievement considering hurling and Gaelic football are still amateur sports.

After you've followed in the footsteps of giants at the Causeway, why not walk a couple of miles down the road to the oldest licensed whiskey distillery in Ireland – **Old Bushmills**. The brewery is visited by over a hundred thousand Irish whiskey fans each year.

The English are not happy
unless they are miserable,
the Irish are not at peace
unless they are at war, and
the Scots are not at home
unless they are abroad.

GEORGE ORWELL

STARS IN OUR EYES

THE ENTERTAINERS WE LOVE

Bray-born graduate of Mathematical Physics and joke-magnet **Dara Ó Briain** has been one of Britain's top-flight stand-up comedians and TV presenters for the past ten years, most notably on the BBC's satirical *Mock The Week*. Alongside comedian Jack Whitehall, Dara has set a new Guinness World Record title for hosting the 'highest stand-up comedy gig in the world', after performing on a British Airways flight in support of Comic Relief. Hopefully the jokes were as smooth as the landing!

Ah, Ireland… That damnable, delightful country, where everything that is right is the opposite of what it ought to be.

BENJAMIN DISRAELI

Since releasing their first hit album *War* in 1983, **U2** have gone on to become the world's biggest rock band, selling an ego-bulging 240 million records. In the 1990s they were Ireland's biggest export, above potatoes and Guinness! The band comprises Larry Mullen, Adam Clayton, The Edge and Bono, who is the only person in history to be nominated for a Grammy, an Oscar, a Golden Globe and the Nobel Peace Prize.

Ireland's newest favourite son, **Chris O'Dowd**, is steadily becoming the toast of Hollywood with films such as *Bridesmaids* (2011) and *The Sapphires* (2012). Hailing loud and proud from Boyle, County Roscommon, O'Dowd's *Moone Boy* TV sitcom is set in his home town and follows the misadventures of a schoolboy and his invisible friend.

Belfast-born **Kenneth Branagh** is one of Northern Ireland's greatest actors, and now a successful director to boot. He has adapted many of Shakespeare's plays to the big screen – his most successful was *Henry V* (1989) for which he was nominated for Best Actor and Best Director – and he also directed the 2011 superhero film *Thor* to much acclaim.

Mary Black is a national treasure and quite possibly *the* voice of Ireland. Born in Dublin, Black is a popular folk and Celtic singer whose voice is purer-than-snow, and very bewitching. She has sung traditional and contemporary Irish songs since the age of eight.

Qui-Gon Jinn. Ra's al Ghul. 'Hannibal' Smith. Michael Collins. Oskar Schindler. Aslan the Lion. Bryan Mills. These are just a handful of the characters whose portrayal has propelled **Liam Neeson** into being one of the biggest Irish actors on the international stage. He is due to receive a Hollywood Walk of Fame star in 2014. Not bad for a lad from Ballymena.

I went to Ireland once…
it was a beautiful country,
and both the women and
men were good-looking.

JAMES CAGNEY

Together, Brian, Nicky, Kian, Mark and Shane made up **Westlife**, Britain's best-selling boy band of all time. Over a period of fourteen years the band sold over 50 million records worldwide and were the first act in history to have their first seven singles all go to Number One in the charts. Their biggest hit, and debut single, 'Swear It Again', sold over 365,000 copies, a record at the time.

He may look perma-grumpy but **Van
Morrison** has a lot to smile about. Born in
Belfast, Van the Man (as his 'Vanatics' call
him) is a Grammy Award-winning Irish
legend. By 2011, Morrison's 1967 hit 'Brown
Eyed Girl' had been played on radio more
than ten million times – that's an average
of 225 times a day for forty-four years!

Being Irish is very much a part of who I am. I take it everywhere with me.

COLIN FARRELL

Born in Dublin in 1951, **Bob Geldof** is
now as much of the Irish furniture as
the Blarney Stone. He was lead singer of
The Boomtown Rats in the seventies and
eighties, and became a household name
around the world as the co-writer of the
charity single 'Do They Know It's Christmas?'
in 1984 and as organiser of the *Live Aid*
charity concert in 1985. He infamously
swore live on TV during the event,
highlighting his fierce passion for the cause
to end the Ethiopian poverty crisis and
prompting millions of people to phone in.

As one-fifth of the boy band One Direction, **Niall Horan** from Mullingar, County Westmeath, has enjoyed mega-success all around the world. Formed live on *The X Factor* in 2010, the band's first album *Up All Night* has been an international success, selling over three million copies to date.

Ireland was a
place for the
renewal of hope
and I still see
it like that.
DANIEL DAY-LEWIS

THE WRITE STUFF

FAMOUS WRITERS, POETS AND PLAYWRIGHTS

Belfast-born **Clive Staples Lewis** is
best remembered for the seven classic
fantasy tales within *The Chronicles of
Narnia*, particularly the much-loved
The Lion, The Witch and The Wardrobe.
Published between 1949 and 1954, the
adventures of Aslan, the Pevensie children
and many other beloved characters
have sold over 100 million copies. How
many of the other six books can you
name off the top of your head?

The 1897 gothic masterpiece *Dracula* introduced the world to the frightening otherworldly horrors of blood-drinking vampire Count Dracula and vampire-hunter Van Helsing. But the novel also introduced its readers to Irish writer **Bram Stoker**, who was born in Clontarf, Dublin, in 1847.

And lucky indeed is the writer
who has grown up in Ireland,
for the English spoken there
is so amusing and musical.

KURT VONNEGUT

Every university student's favourite Irish poet, and winner of the 1995 Nobel Prize for Literature, **Seamus Heaney** was a professor at Harvard University for sixteen years. Considered one of the most revered Irish poets since W. B. Yeats, his first collection of poetry, *Death of a Naturalist,* was published in 1966. Heaney died in August 2013, and the nation mourned.

Born in Dalkey, Dublin, **Roddy Doyle**'s
first, and most famous, novel *The
Commitments* (1987) tells the tale of a
gang of unemployed friends who start
a soul band in Dublin. At times hilarious,
illuminating and tragic, the story inspired
a generation of Irish writers, singers
and artists to 'try a little tenderness'.

Having sold more than 40 million copies of her sixteen published books, the late **Maeve Binchy** is one of Ireland's most popular female writers – and her success made her one of the country's richest women. Her first book, *Light A Penny Candle* (1982), received at the time the largest ever advance sum for a first novel – £52,000.

The Irish are a
fair people; they
never speak well
of one another.

SAMUEL JOHNSON

Sixty years ago, **Samuel Beckett** wrote one of his many literary masterpieces, *Waiting For Godot*; an absurdist play featuring two characters, Vladimir and Estragon, endlessly waiting for someone called Godot to arrive. The drama has been named the most significant English-language play of the twentieth century by the National Theatre of Great Britain. Beckett, from Foxrock, Dublin, won the Nobel Prize for Literature in 1969.

Born in Dublin on 16 October 1854,
Oscar Wilde was as flamboyant as he
was intelligent. A cunning linguist as well
as a master of wit, wordplay and farcical
observations on social class, Wilde's
last witticism was always going to be
fabulous. He remarked on his deathbed:
'My wallpaper and I are fighting a duel
to the death. One or other of us has
got to go!' Truly one of Ireland's sons.

Ireland is rich in literature that understands a soul's yearnings, and dancing that understands a happy heart.

MARGARET JACKSON

Dubliner **Jonathan Swift**'s *Gulliver's Travels* (1726) is a classic of English literature. The shipwrecking of Lemuel Gulliver and his introduction to the tiny townspeople of Lilliput is a bedtime-story favourite and a barbed human satire all rolled into one. If you don't own a copy, you should!

William Butler Yeats was the first – but by no means the last – Irishman to win the Nobel Prize for Literature. Honoured in 1923, Yeats is the much-loved great-great-grandfather of Irish poetry and a leading figure of twentieth-century literature. He famously used his Nobel Prize as a way to express his proud Irishness: 'I consider that this honour has come to me less as an individual than as a representative of Irish literature.'

Of our conflicts
with others we
make rhetoric;
of our conflicts
with ourselves
we make poetry.
W. B. YEATS

Dubliner **George Bernard Shaw** has gone down in history as the only writer to win a Nobel Prize (1925) and an Oscar (1938), the former for his outstanding contribution to literature, the latter for his own screen adaptation of his outstanding play, *Pygmalion*. The screenplay for *Pygmalion* was later adapted into a hugely successful musical, *My Fair Lady*, which you may just have heard of. GBS also founded the London School of Economics, just in case you were failing to be impressed by him!

Ireland, sir, for good or evil, is like no other place under heaven, and no man can touch its sod or breathe its air without becoming better.

GEORGE BERNARD SHAW

And then there's Joyce. **James Joyce** to be precise. This most distinguished of Irish writers, famous for his avant-garde literary techniques, such as the stream of consciousness, was born in Dublin in 1882 and is perhaps best known for his 1922 masterpiece *Ulysses*, as well as *A Portrait of the Artist as a Young Man* (1916) and *Finnegans Wake* (1939).

FOOD FOR THOUGHT

THOUGHT

OUR LANDMARK DISHES

Tayto crisp snacks are a cultural phenomenon across the whole of Ireland. Not only that, but it was Tayto who first invented the flavoured crisp production process, and they were the first to put cooked flavoured potato crisps in a bag. When the Tayto company, owned by Joe 'Spud' Murphy, first set up shop in 1954, they sold 347 packs of their crisps a day. Now they sell 525 packs a minute!

An Irishman was asked if the Irish always answered one question with another.'Who told you that?' he replied.

NIALL TOÍBÍN

On a long, cold night, the perfect nightcap
– sipped and supped all over the world – is
an **Irish coffee**: strong, black, hot coffee,
a pleasing quantity of Irish whiskey (I'll
leave the brand down to you), a spoonful
of brown sugar, topped off with thick
cream (never whipped). Designed to leave
you with a thick creamy moustache, an
Irish coffee is always the best way to end
an evening. Or start the day – up to you!

Only Irish coffee provides in a single glass all four essential food groups: alcohol, caffeine, sugar, and fat.

ALEX LEVINE

The **Ulster fry** is the Northern Irish equivalent to the full English breakfast, with as many of the following as you can fit onto one plate: Irish bacon, sausages, eggs, potato bread, fried tomatoes and soda farls. Not as healthy as a banana, but ten times more delicious.

'**Pooh bear**' is a popular Northern Irish dessert that will hopefully one day cross over to the mainland. Take a few scoops of your favourite creamy ice cream and mix together with big honeycomb chunks sourced fresh from local bees. Sounds great, doesn't it?

The traditional dish **Colcannon** warms
the soul of any Irish person, big or
small. Mashed potato and kale (or
cabbage) mixed together with salt,
pepper and butter – nothing else and
nothing more. If you can sprinkle some
shamrocks over the top as the perfect
garnish, then great – you've got the
true taste of Ireland on your plate.

The Irish don't know what
they want and are prepared
to fight to the death to get it.

SIDNEY LITTLEWOOD

Take some bread and boil it in milk. Add
some cinnamon. Then brown the dish
in the oven. And, there you go; you've
got a **Goody**. Add whipped cream
just to be sure of maximum flavour.
This is a festive dish, popular in parts
of Ireland at Christmas time and on St
John's Eve Bonfire Night (23 June).

Dublin coddle is the Dubliners' weapon
of choice to line their stomachs before
a heavy night out. Sausages, bacon,
onion and potatoes boiled in beef stock.
This will line the stomach and put a
fire in your belly, ready to be doused
by plenty of pints of Guinness.

Crubeens are boiled pigs' feet that are nibbled on as a snack. Crubeens were at their most popular in the 1800s when bacon factories in Cork, Waterford, Limerick, Dublin and Belfast opened up. They are the precursor to modern-day pork scratchings – delicious, salty pig snacks sold at pubs to make you want to drink more!

Brewed at Murphy's Brewery in Cork, **Murphy's stout** may not be widely considered an Irish national drink abroad, but in Ireland it is beloved by many. Guinness's major rival, Murphy's is marketed as the more 'craft' stout of the two, and in 2006 it celebrated 150 years of authentic brewing and is now sold in forty countries.

Ireland is a great
country to die or
be married in.

ELIZABETH BOWEN

MAPPING
THE NATION

OUR WEATHER AND
GEOGRAPHY

Irish hurricane, a flat
calm with drizzling rain.

FRANK CHARLES BOWEN

The island of Ireland is comprised of
two separate (but geographically joined)
states: the Republic of Ireland (made up
of twenty-six counties) and Northern
Ireland, a constituent part of the United
Kingdom (made up of six counties). The
population of the Republic of Ireland
is around 4.5 million; the population of
Northern Ireland, about 1.8 million.

There is no language like
the Irish for soothing
and quieting.

JOHN MILLINGTON SYNGE

The **River Shannon** is the longest river in Ireland. It divides the west from the east and south and is 360 kilometres (224 miles) long. That's almost as long as the entire length of the island of Ireland, which is 486 kilometres (302 miles).

Ireland's largest freshwater lake is **Lough Neagh**. It's 383 square kilometres (148 square miles) in surface area and lies in Northern Ireland, supplying that country with forty per cent of its water. It's also the largest lake in the UK, roughly the same size as the Isle of Wight.

Ireland's highest peak is **Mount Carrauntoohil**, 1,039 metres (3,406 feet) above sea level. The mountain is the central peak of the brilliantly named MacGillycuddy's Reeks range in County Kerry, south-west Ireland.

Ireland is a peaceful country.
And we'll fight anyone
who says otherwise.

RICHARD O'CONNER

The most populated region in Ireland is **Dublin** – the Republic's capital city – with an overall population of around 1.2 million people. In Irish, *Dubhlinn* means 'black pool'.

An Irishman would have been the first to climb Everest but he ran out of scaffolding.

NOEL PURCELL

Powerscourt Waterfall, County Wicklow, is Ireland's tallest and most beautiful waterfall. It has a fierce drop of 121 metres (397 feet). Fed by the River Dargle, the waterfall is also close to the famous Great Sugar Loaf hill.

We may have bad weather
in Ireland, but the sun shines
in the hearts of the people
and that keeps us all warm.

MARIANNE WILLIAMSON

With eleven consonants and eleven vowels, **Muckanaghederdauhaulia** (say that five times fast!) is Ireland's longest place name. It is located in historic County Galway.

You cannot conquer Ireland.
You cannot extinguish the
Irish passion for freedom.

PADRAIG PEARSE

If it weren't for Portugal, Ireland's
Dunmore Head at the tip of the
Dingle Peninsula would be Europe's
westernmost point on the atlas. After
Galway, Ireland's westernmost city, the
next place you'll see is Boston, USA –
4,670 kilometres (2,900 miles) west!

You know it's
summer in
Ireland when the
rain gets warmer.

HAL ROACH

THE OBJECTS OF OUR DESIRE

ICONIC OBJECTS AND FAMOUS INVENTIONS

The Irish have given the world much more than just stout but, as a place to start, **Guinness** is nonetheless a pretty tasty contribution to the world, not to mention the best-selling alcoholic drink of all time. Concocted by Arthur Guinness in the 1770s, this liquid legend is still brewed at the Guinness Brewery in Dublin. Over ten million pints of the 'black gold' are sold proudly every single day in 150 countries around the world, with over three million pints produced at the Brewery each day to meet the demand!

In 1901 John Philip Holland from County Clare designed the world's first operable – and first military-commissioned – **submarine**. Launched in October that year, on its first outing it dived successfully to a depth of 3 metres (10 feet). At 4 metres (13 feet) long, and weighing 2 metric tons (2.25 tons), it was named HMS *Holland I*. Up periscope!

Love is never
defeated, and
I could add,
the history of
Ireland proves it.

POPE JOHN PAUL II

Born in 1857, the very jolly John Joly, from County Offaly, invented two important things: 1) in 1894, by using his special Joly Colour process, he refined **colour photography**; and 2) he devised the first use of **radiotherapy** for use in cancer treatment in 1914, helping save millions of lives. A toast to John Joly!

If you want someone to blame for 'boring' Chemistry lessons at school, then feel free to waggle your finger at Robert Boyle – for it was he who founded **modern chemistry**. His *Sceptical Chemist*, published in 1661, is considered to be a masterpiece of scientific literature, not least because it first explained to people that 'every phenomenon [on earth] was the result of collisions of particles in motion'. Boyle was born in Lismore, County Waterford.

There is no Irish accent. Each county has its own one.

SEÁN O'CASEY

Upon his arrival back in Ireland around
1680, after a trip to Jamaica where he had
observed native people mixing cocoa with
water, Irish physicist Hans Sloane found
a way to mix cocoa with milk instead. In
doing so, he invented **chocolate milk**!

For an Irishman,
talking is a dance.

DEBORAH LOVE

Irish whiskeys – made from fermented grain mash, distilled three times and aged longer than three years in wooden casks – are sipped and savoured all around the world. While Ireland only has five distilleries (Scotland has over a hundred), it is considered by many to be the true home of the world's favourite nightcap. The most popular brand worldwide, Jameson, was first tasted in 1780.

The first person to create the concept of
'**absolute zero**' – the coldest temperature
possible in the universe – was someone
familiar with the concept of feeling the
cold, an Irishman. Belfast-born physicist
William Thomson, 1st Baron Kelvin, will
forever be remembered in the name
given to the unit measurement used to
define absolute temperatures – a kelvin.

As befits an exposed island, fierce gusts of ocean wind regularly batter every corner and crag of the Irish coast. It's no surprise then that an Irishman, Francis Beaufort, devised the **Beaufort wind force scale** – the internationally recognised measure that defines wind speed. Devised in 1805, the scale is much more informative than just shouting, 'it's blowing a hooley out there!'

The **guillotine** is usually associated with the French, right? What if I was to tell you that this gruesome execution device was actually used by the Irish almost five hundred years before the French adopted it? The proof can be found in a painting of a gentleman named Mucod Ballagh, seen using a guillotine-like machine near Merton, County Galway, on 1 April 1307.

In 1889 Irish astronomer William Edward Wilson became the first person to measure the **temperature of the sun**, arriving at an estimation of 6590 ºC; remarkably close to the modern value of 6075 ºC. Knowing the precise temperature of the sun is vital to obtaining a deeper knowledge about the origins of the entire universe.

When Irish eyes
are smiling,
watch your step.
GERALD KERSH

Journalists and secretaries have Monaghan-boy John Robert Gregg to thank for not having sore wrists. It was he who invented **Gregg shorthand** – a method by which words are abbreviated by symbols to help increase the speed and flow of immediate writing for later transcription. Gregg shorthand is different to Pitman shorthand, another variation of the form. Gregg shorthand uses the same thickness in lines throughout but discriminates between similar sounds by the length of the stroke, whereas Pitman shorthand uses line thickness and position to discriminate between two similar sounds.

A LAW UNTO OURSELVES

THE PECULIAR LAWS THAT KEEP US OUT OF TROUBLE

Our Irish blunders are never blunders of the heart.

MARIA EDGEWORTH

In Ireland, it is illegal 'to operate a flashing amber beacon on a range of vehicles such as agricultural tractors'. Laws in most other European countries make those beacons a necessity!

Even when they
have nothing,
the Irish emit
a kind of
happiness, a joy.
FIONA SHAW

It is illegal to perform witchcraft in the city of Dublin: 'Any person who shall pretend or exercise to use any type of witchcraft, sorcery, enchantment, or pretend knowledge in any occult or craft or science shall for any such offense suffer imprisonment at the time of one whole year and also shall be obliged to obscursion for his/her good behaviour.'

The Act of 1310 states that only those
of English race are to be received
into religious orders in Ireland.

The Sunday Observance Act (Ireland) 1695 states: 'And for the better preventing persons assembling on the Lord's Day for such irreligious purposes, tickets sold for money, and any person printing or publishing any such advertisement, shall respectively forfeit the sum of fifty pounds for every such offence to any person who will sue for the same.'

It is illegal to smoke tobacco on Grafton Street, Dublin. (An old, out-of-date and ironic law considering that the street is home to three major tobacconists!)

To be Irish is
to know that
in the end the
world will break
your heart.

DANIEL PATRICK MOYNIHAN

The Tippling Act 1735 prohibits a publican
from pursuing a customer for money owed
for any drink given on credit. (So make sure
all your tipples are paid for on credit!)

A secret in Dublin
just means telling
one person
at a time.

CIARÁN MACGONIGAL

'Any person who carries out, or causes
the carrying out of, a nuclear explosion
in the State shall be guilty of an offense.'
(This 2006 law is applicable to all the UK,
and thank God – we don't want any of
those legal nuclear explosions, do we?)

A layman may drink six pints of ale
with his dinner but a monk may drink
only three. This is so he will not be
intoxicated when prayer-time arrives.
(This one belongs to early Irish law,
often referred to as Brehon law, which
comprised the statutes that governed
everyday life in early medieval Ireland.)

Maradona great.
Pelé better.
George Best.
POPULAR IRISH PHRASE

THERE'S
NO PLACE
LIKE HOME

FAMOUS PLACES TO SEE
AND THINGS TO DO

The oldest pub in Ireland – and therefore the best place to have a pint of Guinness – is **The Brazen Head**, located on the south bank of the River Liffey in Dublin. This boozer opened its doors in 1198 and is beloved by all for its lively atmosphere (especially after a few pints). As James Joyce once said, 'You get a decent do at The Brazen Head.'

Ireland's ruins are
historic emotions
surrendered to time.

HORACE SUTTON

In a small town called Downpatrick, County Down, lie the remains of the nation's patron saint, St Patrick. They lie in a place of quiet worship in **Down Cathedral** and are worth a visit if you're in nearby Belfast – the gravesite is only 20 miles away.

Christ beside me, Christ before me, Christ behind me, Christ within me, Christ beneath me, Christ above me.

SAINT PATRICK

One of the more bookish things to do in Dublin is to take a **James Joyce-themed walking tour** of the city. Follow in the famous footsteps of Leopold Bloom and walk the route he takes in the 'Lestrygonians' episode of Joyce's masterpiece *Ulysses*. En route you can also stop off at many of the locations mentioned in the stories in *Dubliners*.

Despite being dubbed the 'most unhygienic tourist attraction in the world', the kissing of the mystical **Blarney Stone** at Blarney Castle, near Cork, is a proud Irish tradition. As the legend goes, anyone who kisses this stone is endowed with a great sense of humour, wit and charm – not that the Irish need any more than they already have. Millions of people from around the world have visited this tourist site over the past 200 years.

Take a trip to **Inishbiggle**, a small island off the coast of County Mayo and home to just twenty-two people at the time of writing. Your challenge: to meet the entire population! Off you go…

May the enemies of Ireland never eat bread nor drink whiskey, but be afflicted with itching without the benefit of scratching.

IRISH PROVERB

With more than 2,500 clubs, **Gaelic football** is one of Ireland's favourite amateur sports. The top three winners of the GAA All-Ireland Football Championship are Kerry (36 times), Dublin (24) and Galway (9). If you get a ticket to a Kerry-Dublin final at Croke Park you are in for a treat!

If you're lucky enough to be Irish, then you're lucky enough.

GRACE BOYLE

The **Dublin Literary Pub Crawl** is the most famous of all Dublin pub-crawls – and that's saying something! As the evening's jovial tour guides take you on a walkabout of many of the city's literary hotspots, they will perform extracts from the finest works of some of Dublin's pre-eminent writers, including Joyce, Beckett, O'Brien and Wilde.

The town of **Dingle**, at the foot of the
Slievanea mountain, is one of the most
popular tourist attractions in Ireland. Dingle
is alive with Irish culture and character and,
because the Dingle peninsula is the most
westerly point of Ireland, visitors are treated
to two extreme vistas in one panorama
– mountains behind them and 3,000
miles of raging ocean in front of them.

Do you not feel that this island is moored only lightly to the seabed, and might be off for the Americas at any moment?

SEBASTIAN BARRY

Described by Oscar Wilde as a 'savage beauty', **Connemara** is, to many, the real emerald in Ireland. Sitting at the very edge of Europe, Connemara is a completely unspoilt landscape. It is also the nation's sporting paradise; a place where you can golf, fish, cycle, walk, horse ride, rock climb, scuba dive, sail, swim and bog snorkel with the most spectacular views in the country.

Once banned by the British for being too nationalistic, **hurling** is Ireland's oldest (and toughest!) field game, believed to be over 3,000 years old. Each team has fifteen players and there are seven officials to keep control of proceedings as players use their hurleys in an attempt to launch the sliotar (a small cork ball covered in leather) at breakneck speed between the posts. Catch a game during the February–September season at any one of the forty-three Gaelic Athletic Association stadiums around the country.

In Ireland every place you
visit and every person
you meet has a story…
you will never be bored.

MAEVE BINCHY

If you're interested in finding out more about our books, find us on Facebook at **Summersdale Publishers** and follow us on Twitter at **@Summersdale**.

www.summersdale.com